That Motley Drama !

Poetry by

Daniel Sokoloff

Contents

That Motley Drama!

Conversation in a Bar Off-Broadway

They tell me I'm musical,
but trust me here,
I don't sing.
There's magic in my hands,
but my wand doesn't wave at the band,
doesn't bleed, and it doesn't speak,
it just writes.

There's a spectacle in my head,
I've been dreaming of it for decades now,
like a ballet/Broadway style musical hybrid thing,
this big, beautiful disaster kind of show,
a real event, like that Spider-man musical those idiots made,
but with this whole personal, universal story holding it up,
kind of thing everyone can relate to.
It's the story of a little kid trying to win his dad's respect,
only he's this little demon kid, with bat ears and massive black eyes,

like, there's this huge song and dance number that'll bring you to tears.
You think Peter Jackson's *Lord of the Rings* movies had backstory?
We'll get the stage lights to shine blue, it'll be like freaking heaven,
and there will be burning angels falling in complicated spirals.
We'll have Adele or someone singing all mournful over harp music
while these demon brute guys twirl and leap around the stage,
they'll be these baroque singers, and they'll get louder and louder
'till that harp is drowned out and the blue lights'll turn all red and black,
and then
WHAM!

Scene transition! Back to our little demon hero! He's sword fighting
his dad in a castle,
and he's backstabbed by his best friend, and as he's dying his dad and
his mentor reveal that they betrayed him, set him up as a martyr, and
we'll actually throw him to the audience,
all covered in glitz and fake blood, and
then our female lead will come out this trap door that we'll build right
in the aisle,
she'll be this cute innocent thing called
the Mosquito Queen
and she'll have this like spotlight on her as she sings,
and then all those burning angels'll show up again, and they'll be
harmonizing, singing in this like
perfectly tuned trance-like thing,
and he'll wake up, right, and I forgot, he's a little bat demon,
but get this, he was born WITHOUT WINGS!
and like, the Mosquito Queen, she gives him a second shot at life,
y'know she wants to be avenged,
and our hero, we've got this little kid on stage playing him now,
and it's like he's with the audience in the aisle,
seeing his entire life playing out before him,
and he sees the life he lost, this little kid looking up to his dad
while the world burned and suffered,
sees him crying without knowing why,
it's like he's been living on the margins of every day,
accomplishing nothing and not ever mattering,
and now he gets it, dude,
it's, fuck, the word,

catharsis,
and as those dead angels start singing again,
these big black batwings burst from his back,

and he fucking flies!

it'll be the most epic thing you've ever seen in your entire life,
and he'll meet his father,
and he'll say something like,
"I'll never be like you,"
Or
"I'm above your judgement now,"
or something
and then he'll die, or fly into the moonlight
or something,
and then curtains;

I could write it,
I've got the whole thing in front of me,
it's like a ghost in my bones.

The Ice-Man

Always in the dark, unable to sleep,
the Ice-Man dances madly, lost in the void.
Eyes of fire blazing in the freezing waste,
his loneliness as the original creature is complete.
There is a rainbow bridge somewhere in the blue veil,
sometimes, after a rainy day you can see it,
but it can never be reached by mortals such as us,
for the Ice-Man's skull was placed over our dust-ball world,
a cosmic condom to protect us from splendor
we can never hope to conceive of.

We talk of love as though it were a small thing,
but you are my anchor in this drab world,
for the thoughts the Ice-Man fills me with
overwhelm and threaten to drown me in madness.
Your flesh is warm, your kisses are strong,
ruining my conviction, stealing my love.
I need your greed, your addiction to my attention,
for with these narcotic thorns in my soul,
I shall not bury myself again,
seeking secrets hidden in the clouds.
A fly caught in your honey,
I gaze at the drifting stains in the sky
that were once the brains of the Ice-Man.

I've rung your doorbell,
but suddenly I can only think of that misty realm
where no flowers grow.
Stretched between two extremes,

murderer gods gloating in the sky,
flowers within my hand,
I collapse,
stretched like never before, sobbing,
for I hear the Ice-Man's kin drowning in his blood,
raining from the cracked void,
the Ice-Man's head torn from his spine;.

Oh darling, won't you put on some music
and help me drown out these voices I hear?
There are psychic maggots feasting on the current in my head,
and over and over I think the same thought,
"The Ice-Man's broken body was made into the world."
Do you think it is possible
that we could all be made into planets,
balls of bone,
blood drifting into space like some nightmare ribbon?

The sugar of your scent so close to me
makes me think of our anatomy,
coiled up behind our soft mortal shells,
and then without a doubt,
I realize that all the world could be art
if only we could peel off our skin
and paint the walls
with our blood.

Free, Just Like That Bluebird

The Next Day,
I sat in the pub
all alone, just me and my
cold tumbler of beer,
its decal
of the mighty Thor
shimmering obscenely in
the pubs half-twilight.

I sipped it.
"Hello, old friend," I
said to that dark, acrid beer.
Newtown is so quiet,
these giants
never knew what hit
them. Yesterday hurt, today
is Unbearable.

It happened.
Blackstar was laid Low.
I spent half the day crying,
but when night fell, I
tasted of ash on my tongue.
My iPod
felt small in my hand;

Apple's best
invention, it seemed
to be made of durable,

Indestructible
steel, so strong
I believe now it will
outlive all of my Heroes.
Tonight I shattered

my silence.
I took my Heathen
tumbler in one hand, hammer
dangling from my neck,
for Hours
meditating Outside, until
the riot of ice

at the pub
made me think, "Let's Dance."
Now sitting alone, I feel
that I'm a pretty
bad gay poet;
but then again, so
was Ziggy.

Morning Star

I remember how it was;
thy shadow fell, and we knew again
of the light; long ago they tore
our soft bodies away from that glen
where comfort and joy were rule and right,
and the light was all around, stupefying and holy.
So the legends say, and if I trust my sight,
there is nothing of that light here, only a melancholy
progression of seasons, a struggle for purpose,
and the revolution of the stars, glinting proof
that we are not alone on this hungry surface.
You have always told us the truth,
was it not you in the glen, seducing us
with your gift to perceive?
When the fiery wheel kicked dust
in its pursuit of us, did you grieve?

The idolatry we gave you, oh Lord,
it was not sufficient, though you did revel
in our puny attempts to honor the blood poured
from your body when you earned that poor title: Devil.
How lost we were when the snow came,
and the sun was missing in the sky
as clouds massed, and the beasts inflamed
with hunger sought us with burning eye.
Unwanted and doomed,
you showed us the spear, gave us the first spark,
saying, "You'll figure it out, I assume,
else truly perish," and your smile was stark

as we studied these, and learned to forage,
to kill, to cooperate, to reign.
We grew in thy image,
and our cities would not be
if not for thy chains.

We are mighty now,
and perhaps we have forgotten that first meeting,
when you commanded us to never bow,
and taught us how to keep the night retreating
from our prideful march towards ascendance.
We stare, study, love, and fight from bubbles
and fortresses, scattered throughout the firmament
we once marveled at. Though our troubles
are handled by mechanical angels,
your temples are now but dust,
we are far from graceful,
and into Lethe you have been thrust.
But I see your eyes when I dream,
smoldering like supernovas,
and I know that we will not reconvene,
for, Morning Star, you have always been with us.

Gabby,
(Or the Dissection of an Angel)

"The one you love and the one that loves you are never, ever, the
same person."
-Chuck Palahniuk

I: Gross Anatomy Lesson

Gabby, my sad one, how is your skin still so soft?
Your wings droop on the edges of the table,
they cast such a dramatic shadow, the shapes so pronounced,
like razors slashing my eyes.
All things should weep for you, my expired beauty,
soon to be returned, in agony to your mortal ashes.

Gabby, my cruel one, why did you long for a lonely death?
Your sweetly-formed mouth hangs open,
do you have more harsh words for me?
The scalpel hangs in the air, wavers just above your pallid flesh.
Your kisses were soft and yielding, cotton candy or bubble gum,
and your smile was extinct,
you only ever talked of misanthropy and lovelessness.

You were weary of endless nihility,
but there were too many smiles in the world,
even the broken things were showing their rotten teeth.
There was no hope for understanding anymore,
time to molt our skin and become terrible things,
scabbed wings, red compound eyes, no context for our misery,
never any reasons given, no prayers from each other,

none offered, none given.
Get me a bowl of sugar, I'm going in.

Gabby, why did you abuse yourself so violently?
Your lost gaze entreats me, even in death,
do you blame me for your damage?
Was it my rough hug that fractured your ribs, punctured your lungs?
Gabby, my Gabby, you would have torn out my heart
just as surely as I would have given it to you.

Why did you listen to them?
Those unkillable shapes, they thought it was cute when you sniffled,
and delighted in the scars you dug into your body,
digging for endorphins with a serrated knife.
You groped in the dark for a hug,
the debutante of pain, and they seized on you,
no worries about where you hatched,
they took you until this place was meaningless,
silhouettes of dogs, whispers of trees,
black waters, lone and still,
and the Worm bawling and bawling.

Should I sew you back up?
There's nothing left inside your small body;
I remember you, a small girl chasing green will-o'-the-wisps,
you'd lopped off your galactic hair to spurn another man,
and you were paying for all your own drinks,
mocking the elves who fled here,
chocking on the toxic fumes that bubbled from the mud.

II: The Vigil

I'll slip off your skin to reveal the ruined ridges of your ribs,
further confirming my identity as your worst enemy.

Love is just a word we threw around,
drunk and arguing the virtues of deicide.

Staring out the window shouldn't be this hard,
I need to get out, need to get some mud on these boots.
A girl smokes a cigar at the club down the street,
not sure how that makes me feel.
Smoking girl, girl smoking,
faded impression of eyes too happy to cry;
it's too close to the morning to be thinking so clearly.

She loved driving with the sunrise,
always fleeing one bed for another distraction.
She hated sleeping alone, the wind howling against the window,
her body aching, shaking apart.
Everything was a boring old cliché to her aborted heart.

I'm so low now, gazing at the merry lights across the still water,
now I can see how she was so easily distracted;
the voids between the brightness are too deep,
far too deep to ignore.
I see not just the lights reflected in the water,
but also my own face,
and my own eyes meet:
there is nothing to learn there,
and I realize the folly of our own attention.
These failures to connect, to love, to understand
befall us because we never listen,
never calm down and look the ones we love in the eyes
and feel their pain for ourselves.

Enjambment

At what point can I run off
from all this
into the
wilderness
free to be
barefoot
to starve and
die
and hide my
naked flesh
from the cold
all on my own time?

I Hate My Wallet

I bought it at Hot Topic years ago on clearence,
it was only 20¢,
that's pretty much why I bought it.
I didn't care about the little Jack Skellington heads,
grinning, smirking, grimacing, and laughing all over it,
it was cheap, and I needed a new goddamn wallet.
It's almost so lame it's ironic, something
a teenager would carry,
especially now that it's so beat up and dirty.
I wish I would just grow the fuck up and buy a nicer,
[more manly]
bifolding one, made of sleek black leather
that smells like new shoes and has a special clear pocket for my
driver's license,
a sexy black executive style wallet, with all the bells and whistles,
like RFID protection and an extra insert for pictures of my family and
a change purse for the quarter I carry for an Aldi cart.
Thing is, as much as I feel like I ought to upgrade,
every time I pick up a new wallet,
I wonder why I would spend $15 or $20 on a new one
when I could just keep that cash in my old,
perfectly functional one.

The Melodia Cycle

Aurora

Together we tumble
into the sky.
Down below a whale
calls fearfully to her young,
and you bite your lip,
your fury evoking Athena,
as we strive.
Transfixed
when you stood on
your
tiny toes
I forgot who I was
for too long
and then you
flipped my world,
and I seized you
and dragged you down
into the heartless sky
with me.
We're like falling eagles
indifferent to velocity,
powerless to let go
unwilling to disengage
until I end you with a jab,
stabbing you again and again
until my sword slips.
Your blood and passion streams
across the voracious sky
in a splatter of rainbow light.

I hit the ground,
a halo of dust choking me
as I watch your auroras ripple above,
the vibrant tendrils rippling
like a tattered flag.

Genesis

"She burns like the sun
I can't look away
she'll burn our horizons
make no mistake."
-Muse, "Sunburn"

Born beneath his septenary glare,
my heart was synchronized,
wired to beat along with the pulse
of the Great Red Dragon's bad heart.

We toiled in the hollow heart of the world,
where our melancholy songs echoed like prayers,
laying carefully each brick and column,
smelting with our repressed passions
the bars and chains
of the Great Red Dragon's kingdom of suffering.

For ages uncounted,
my subterranean kind slaved
and perished in the black of that hollow place,
unmourned, never dreaming of anything
until the ceiling splintered,
and the rapturous daylight
smote the weak eyesight of the Great Red Dragon.

Beings seemingly composed of nothing
but holy fire grappled and swore,
wounding one another and swearing

damnation, even as the molten hatred
of the Great Red Dragon, furious at being awoken,
swept them away,
purging their heavenly essences,
quelling their righteous wrath
to a single, feeble, nihilistic twang.

Only one of those fallen stars remained, Darling,
and that was you, born to dazzle every vista
with your splendor; taking the burning sun
for your battle armor, nothing infernal or earthly
could stay your onslaught,
save for the Great Red Dragon, who remembered
the glory of his lost cause.

You were cast out,
expelled like magma, your rage
drowned in the sea.
We pulled you back, fearful lest the brightest,
most beautiful thing in all Creation
should burn out,
never to exist again in the world,
but to our dismay,
the Great Red Dragon,
with hellish plumes of black flame bursting from his nostrils,
ordered us to seal you away,
to trap you like a butterfly.

Broken-hearted between my beloved lord
and the downed angel who would have been
Queen of Heaven and all the Hollow Earth,
I severed my cord to the Great Red Dragon,
and flew into the golden sunbeam

that lingered still from where you, my beloved,
the angel Melodia,
shattered my idea of what the world was
and the limits
of the sky.

Paladin

She huddled in that dark hollow,
ankles bound with cruel weights,
glaring with rage and shame
as the sun, free of her word of power,
spun away, abandoning her
naked form
to the dark hollow of the earth.

I listened to gentle clink of her collar,
helpless as what
remained of her holy fire
was quenched from her beautiful form
and she was forced into a crystalline cell,
her wings bound against her in rings of steel;
I could bear it no longer,
and turned away in sorrow.

I considered my umbilical wire,
binding me to the will of my
King and Country.
Seas of magma hissed,
a hush fell over the chittering nether bats,
and several of my fellow bottom-dwellers
turned on me in horror
as I tore it, tears spilling from eyes
that had been cursed
by a glimpse of Heaven's light.

Suddenly, the surface was calling to me,
and the hollow earth fell away

in clouds of dust and
drops of blood;
my fallen angel's sobs drove me on,
and I climbed, dogged as a pilgrim,
scraping my way away from
the black netherworld,
where far below
the screams of my brethren,
begging me to stay in the safety
of the darkness
scarred me.

The world was so beautiful…
my wires dragged,
raw and hungry,
desperate for a connection.
I crawled through the forest,
clinging to the earth
for fear that
I would fall into the sky,
for there was no ceiling.

Shedding my scales,
soon I was exposed and alone,
and I cried out, for
the thread of light
that had led me out of the hollow
had withered.
I lay down on a riverbank,
soothed by the battered moon's
weak light, and slept.

I was awoken by the vanguard of dawn,
trumpeting all the world with its gaudy light,

and I was hysterical with joy
to see the bauble of my love
unharmed, blazing as though
it had never been drowned in the ocean.
"Melodia," I whispered to myself,
and the sparks of my elation
turned to ashes.

The sun, burning as if it were
invincible, was nothing but
a sphere of raging fire,
without my beloved angel
to fill its hollow fury with her
divine grace.
The colors and
sounds of the morning
did nothing to lighten
the heavy notes of my sorrow;
I was alone.

Meandering, I came at last
to an odd cave
where the pull of some great force
relentlessly drew me towards it.
I walked a hidden path that my
underworlder senses told me true
that no living creature had tread
in centuries.

The cavern gave way,
as all things do.
I stood before a wrought gate
that was overtaken with the greenest ivy

and where the branches of primeval trees
hung like prisoners,
fruits dangling like supplications.
The scent of loam and fresh water
was overwhelming, and I could hear
bees and the chatter of beasts
from deep within the hidden garden.

The world was so beautiful,
but the garden before me
was unearthly. The vibrant greenery
and fertility of its life
was untouched, and hollow,
like the sun above
without my beloved
to add her luster to its fire.

My quest had been one of folly,
and I knew then,
that there was nothing for me
in all the world
than to return then to the hollow,
to toil in the dust and blackness.
I had been a fool
to long for that lovely creature,
to see and understand her
dreams for the heavens.

Hark! A piteous cry made me stop,
and I drew closer to the garden.
A man lay, his white habit
foul with filth and vomit.
"Don't go," he pleaded,

and as I knelt, I felt
deep in my wires
as he expired.
At his side, a sword blazed,
a fantastically forged weapon,
its metal humming with spiritual wrath.
Double-edged and massive, it
could only have been forged
by the hand and fire
of a god.

It whispered to me,
and I saw the first man and woman
driven from that place by its terrible fury.
The blade's metal vibrated with sorrow;
faith in its wielder, faith for its forger
made it feel
but it was alone now,
defending a forgotten garden
from dead men.
My thoughts of Melodia drew the blade
towards me, and with a hiss of passion,
I seized its hilt.

I lost the ground,
consumed by mystical radiation
that charred my soul, and
prodded my heart
with desperate needles.
The intelligence that was seared
into the sword's core
asked me for the object of my faith,
and I could feel its will

shredding me down to my
most basic,
burning me out
and I thought of that lone,
doomed ray of light,
the angel lying helpless,
at the mercy of the Great Red Dragon,
and as the agonized weapon
clutched in my claws
vaporized me,
I uttered her name,
"Melodia, angel of glory and light,
Queen of all Heaven and the Hollow Earth."

The sword spun in my hands,
the sky turned from blue
to black and airless
and the earth seemed
naught more than a puny,
blue, cloudy orb,
to be shattered with a punch;
I turned around and around,
blazing so bright,
even the sun kept its distance.
Laughing as I exulted in my new power,
I dropped back to the world,
my faith and love
carrying me back
though I longed to unlock the beautiful secrets
that hid behind the stars;
I knew that within the Hollow Earth,
the greatest star of all awaited.

Faith Binder

"Yea, though I walk through the valley of the shadow of death,
I will fear no evil,
for thou art with me;
thy rod and thy staff, they comfort me."
-Psalm 23:4

I am in your shadow.

Your silver wings fill the sky,
and the holy radiance of your fire
blots out the arrogant sun
as you descend.
Enfolded in your snowy arms
and queenly legs,
I whisper your name,
gasping as our lips lock
and your Heavenly light
fills me,
waking me, saving me,
remaking me.

Your divine favor glows on my chest,
and my sacred sword,
tempered on Heaven's darkest day,
and blooded on the proudest angel,
returns to my hand.
"Faith Binder," you murmur,
looking into my soul
with eyes that have turned

archfiends into poets.
So the blade is named,
for only by his faith in
Heaven's mighty ruler
could its original wielder
have felled dread Satan.

"Melodia,"
I sigh,
"Most beautiful and loved
of all the angels of
Heaven or Hell,
what man would not throw
down his weapon
and open his heart for you?"

Up, up, and away,
into the wrath of skies
that will soon be yours,
we hurtle,
just as we did so long ago,
battling like Satan and Michael;
Your aurora explodes behind us,
an exquisite bruise upon the firmament,
and all the world
cowers before the lightning
that crowns your sooty hair.

Melodia

I kneel, helpless before your radiance.
You consume me,
my arms, my legs, my entire body,
my pitiful soul, like a candle in the wind,
every atom and spark of my existential existence
is forfeit to your magnificence.

I have no choice,
you are a remorseless sun
searing my junkyard heart.
There is no mercy,
the rust and hatred, scorched,
falls from me in meteoric showers,
and framed against the peaceful oblivion
of your universal dreams,
I am reborn.

Cynicism dies.
My black-forged chains cannot survive
the persistence of your pride,
and I am freed to follow you,
my demonic wrath
the flowering star in your
thunderous, ebony crown.

I suffer and die to bring you glory,
and you
raise me from the swill of lost souls,
your electric touch,

a divine caress,
your kiss of life,
the hammer-fall of grace.

Donald Trump,
Goblin President

Coronation

I watched the boldest,
the richest fools our country had to offer
gather in their moot,
all to declare to each other, and maybe to us,
why they should lead us, and no one else.
Hypocrites and sociopaths the lot of them,
business as usual, but something unexpected happened:
a goblin snuck in.

Grey clouds gather,
and I try to tell myself
that they are just the envoys of winter.
All this, the freezing winds,
the threat of cities buried in snow,
the absent sun,
it's just winter as usual.

There's a part of me that wants to relax,
just take it easy and ignore the news
the way so many ignored the election,
but the politics don't feel abstract now.
The goblin has dredged up the nastiest
ideas, set the politics of identity to war,
and now even looking in the mirror
reveals a complicated spiral.
I'm bisexual, but I've got white skin,
maybe that means I'll make it through this era alive;
But then again, most Jews pass for white, until the men
robed like ghosts remind us that

no, we aren't white after all.
I never thought I would be like this, so
political.

Fear is corrosive,
and we've all caught it,
even those who cheered as the goblin
shouted down the career politicians,
and danced the fiery dance that so many angry people
felt for their common man.
Fear is the reason we're turning on one another;
I would say it's like a wildfire, but that isn't right.
It's more like a catchy tune you hear,
one you hate, but it's so simple and persistent,
so prevalent, there's really no avoiding it, and eventually
you can't get it out of your head, no matter how hard you try,
and before you know it,
when some goblin steps forward to accept
a crown that is far too heavy for his neck to support,
and they play that catchy tune,
you find yourself nodding along with it,
and as the fluffy, obliterating snow falls,
a touch of warmth.

Dissociative

They tell me that a goblin will be our president now,
and as he screeches his plans for the future of our nation,
I find that I cannot see the faces of my friends anymore.
A worm gnaws at the sinews of my heart,
and I feel so sick from his mischief.
There is no comfort when so many
remained silent
as the bonfires lit by the goblin's supporters
thawed comatose dragons
and delivered our future
into their scaly hands.

My mother once said,
as she twisted a spoon into a ring,
that one could make art out of anything,
if only they had the vision.
I wonder if these former friends of mine
ever considered what their inaction
allowed.

Our verdant gardens withered,
malicious winds tore our bridges apart,
and pink worms fell like hail stones,
showering those they touched with despair and madness.
There was no clear way to slow the crisis,
so we ignored it,
and hoped it would go away.

After the election,
the rain cast the decaying leaves to the ground,
and I saw a blue "I'm with Her!" placard
disintegrate as a man pulled it off his car.
He looked angry, shivering in the cold
and when our eyes locked, I realized
that I had once known him.

Nihilist Fever

This nation is sick, and
I might have it too,
this nihilist fever
that is making America
want to die.
I think of Superman
withdrawing,
tired from pursuing his Truth & Justice
and whatever that third thing was
and just feel tired.
I want to clean the stains
from our flag,
but now Donald Trump
is holding it now,
and isolation and hatred seem to be
the biggest hits on the airwaves right now.

They tell me to relax,
the goblin whom I must accept
as president
is obsessed with space travel.
They tell me
he will take us to Mars,
but I can't relax
when I know that
the first building we put there
will be a church.

The sun is shining, and the ascendance
of regressive morals
are reminding me that soon
I might burn like a flag.

Crazy Town

Driving the divide from our side of 95
to the suburban side,
I feel like I've got a millstone stuck in my head.
Chatter on the radio reminds me
that a part of my culture
is the belief that the ability to own weapons of war
is a "God-Given Right."

I try to focus on the better aspects of this society,
decent highways, access to clean water,
discount outlets, mostly free speech,
but then sometimes,
listen to a talk radio station
that I refer to as "Crazy Town,"
where edgy winners
babble about the culture wars
that they're losing
I think
(we did elect a goblin as president).

They're particularly bad
whenever a school shooting happens.
One of these weapons, legally purchased,
background checks passed,
enters a school
and shoots unarmed children,
and then these shock jocks posing as intellectuals
scream about the mental health epidemic
and suggest we arm the teachers.

They frame it as an issue of Liberty
with a capital "L",
invoking the Star Wars fantasy of
resisting a tyrannical government,
like their little guns will do anything
against Hellfire missiles.

It's crazy, and it makes me sick
because while they're ranting about
the second amendment like it's some holy writ,
I'm thinking of my pretty little sister,
chubby, blue-eyed Yaffa,
and a bullet breaking her forehead,
spattering her brains on the wall,
and those NRA fucks,
who've been waiting all their lives
for someone to take their guns away
and remember that Crazy Town
isn't constrained to the radio.

American Carnage

I saw it in a Dunkin' Donuts,
the kind you can find anywhere
in America.
It was on a TV you can buy
anyplace that sells electronics,
and I was eating a
terrible turkey sandwich,
the kind you can only get
at Dunkin' Donuts.
I had the misfortune of seeing
a goblin
sworn in as the president of my country,
a sorrow I shared with millions of others,
but they didn't share my misfortune
of a terrible turkey sandwich.

"We share one heart,
one home, and one
glorious destiny,"
croaked the goblin,
who, I was told the next day,
had been angered that he couldn't have
missiles and tanks marching
in his inaugural parade.

I finished my sandwich, chewing the
awful meat, knowing full well
that if I didn't eat it,
I would suffer from hunger

back at work
as much as I understood that there
would be no freak assassinations,
no fortuitous appearance of any messiahs,
just a light chill, and soft rain.

America runs on Dunkin',
so the corporate byline states.
I suspect that is partially true,
as I'm an American worker,
and I'm in there all the time.
But it seems to me that America also runs on
foreign wars, oil, and cheap labor, among
other first-world vices.
The goblin talked about our cities
and schools, our economy,
called it all
"American carnage,"
but overseas,
those two words mean something
very different.

Political Machine

"It's time to start the engine,"
Bernie thinks as he sifts the ground coffee
into the flimsy white filter,
so many grounds like smooth,
beautiful, black grains of sand.
Time to draft the email
that will be sent from an automated account
to millions of American
spam folders
in his digital rolodex.

Behind Bernie,
the President gestures on the television,
manic and massive and
orange as a prison suit.
No time to clean his glasses
as the cooling fan on his laptop whirrs
and the coffee drips,
no time even to stir in the
heavy white cream.

"This time will be right,
last time was all wrong,"
Bernie mutters,
his watch ticking glumly.

Decimator

Ange de L'Aviation

He was a man as square as the god he spurned,
and I appeared before him with a message
from "On High,"
but he coveted my figure divine,
and uttered the holy syllables of my true name,
stealing from me my power and agency.

The circle's chalk lines trapped my light,
and the crystal he held sealed me in bronze.
The propellers and engines that were my thrones
went dead,
and my black wings hardened at my back.

I can't even cry from the horror,
dreaming of the rebel angels,
swallowed by the void so may eons ago;
their terrified screams echoed through our
storming realm, and our sorrow at their fate
didn't dissipate even when
we heard their pain turn to rebellious screams of defiance.

Elfs and demons fill the sanctum of my captor.
He has forgotten me,
a burning seraph bearing the gift of flight for mankind,
trapped like a hapless fly.

My Lord, you will not forgive me for this,
but if my tongue were not turned to bronze,
I still would not sing for your mercy.

Why would you let your beautiful, loyal child
endure the misery of stagnation?

Should I forgive your indifference?
When the calcium of my bones
stains the grey below me,
will my angel brothers sing of your love?

Sweet Satan, I know of your agony now.
You burned above us, the brightest star in our celestial sky,
and yet you were alone,
a monstrance blazing for the credit of an alien intelligence.
I watch my captor teach his little son
how to keep an angel in chains,
and I can't even cry from the horror.

I can't even cry from the horror.
Sad Satan, you who showed the cherubs
the joys of corporeal shapes,
and taught the heavenly choirs the song of independent thought,
only you in your dark kingdom could understand;
if you should catch a glimpse of me in my sorry state,
offer me a blast from your infernal tin,
so furious and sad
that the pearly gates feel the wind of your trumpet.

Meltdown

I can't keep the shape in my heart
together;
the imprint of a fetal dragon
sleeping as it waits
to be born again,
incubated by the psychic heat
of the epiphany I can't escape,
falling apart in my own shadow.

Steam billows from the corners of my mouth,
flames cooking the meat
on my bones from deep within.
It'll all be over soon,
but I'm losing touch with everything that matters,
nose is gone already
and I can't ignore
the whimpering, scaly slug in my chest.

It wants to be born,
nurtured in the ruination of my being,
born in the immolation of my intrinsic self.
Red light, chunky and thick in the
night's empty ribcage
splatters across the dirty snow
like wine splashed on a wedding dress,
and I feel the alien soul
bellowing for my charity.

What can I do?
I'm melting down like
Godzilla,
leaking destructive light,
a frail angel obliterating my domain
as I shatter apart,
trying to maintain my integrity
as unwanted changes
are wrought on the form
I thought belonged to me,
was me.

The colors of my despair,
the tenor of my terror and defiance
scar the daemon
its eyes turn to exes, its mouth a bottomless pit
and its wings razors that will shred the world.
I lose the sounds first, and then the colors,
and then the sense of corporeality
as I am broken down,
sucked dry for nourishment
and scattered by the night wind,
whispering mysteries to me
as the dark red glare
gets smaller and smaller
until it's just another winking star
in the distant field of black and silver.

A Girl Named Hell

Awoken by the demure
singing of the cat bells,
she strode to her great
curved window
and touched the glass with a skeletal hand.
Longing in mortification for her glance,
her lightless queendom swirled far below,
mists hanging like
empty ghouls stretched
and hung on the wind,
a titanic rock formation
carved in crude reverence
to her crown of horns.

Her leather robe
could not quiet
her living heart,
which gasped obscene as she departed
from the sensual coils
of her castle walls.
She fluttered above
the waters of the river Gjöll,
where the dashed
dreams of the dead
glittered
like the stars in the sky
she yearned after in dreams.

A massive root hung from the roof
of the Underworld,
black and twisted, and
the lonely Queen rested in its
thick sinews and placed her hands
on her face; far above,
she could just hear the distant
pitter-patter of a savage rain.

Troegenator

The double bock demon hangs like a bat,
dangling from crumpled wings.
he's seen a lot,
only a sneer to show for all he's done.

He's my bad influence pal,
chilling on my sinking dreams as I wait around,
too worn down to feel desperate,
just faintly hoping the bus to paradise pulls in.

[The ditch runs deep]
I've got a beard that I've lost control of,
my other friends call it the "wizard beard",
but it isn't cool.
Scruffy, greasy, I'm like an embarrassing hobo wizard,
but the demon doesn't care.
His beard is a royal forest,
the powerhead of the wild mask of his face.
The pagan fury of his bestial sneer
stifles any pretenses or restraints you might have
as he pours the cold beer,
stomps his hooves against the wooden floor.

Quoth the demon:
"Hell, you gonna mop helplessly at the gore like a little bitch all night?
You gonna drag your bony ass all the way up Golgotha?
For what? Fuck it man,
drink that black stuff,
fill your empty soul with my liquid grains,

its smooth, slick notes will dull the sting of your failure.
Change, catharsis, death, rebirth,
take it from one whose ridden the lightning
and been swallowed whole by the wolf;
it's better to drink until the alcohol scars your liver
and you collapse in a puddle of mud,
trampled by all the cruelty that forever rules the earth.
Existence is a wild hog that one only masters in his mind,
it bucks you off when its finished toying with you,
and your name is lost to the whirlwind of oblivion."

Dog

They said my fur was fine
Dress me in silks
I'd win prizes

I don't chase the cars
I'm thin and my bones creak
This pain is my reward

Chain link throws me back
Bruises me,
I feel rabid

My teeth tremble
Gums soft and vulnerable
It aches inside

They fed me scraps
And when I shit in the house
They beat my skinny hide

I howl
At night, I howl
As only a dog might

Bound, I hunger
All I see are prey
It aches inside

I'm still so close
To being tame
You might think I'm safe

I'm a good boy
As long as I get my
Mouthful

It aches inside
I want the hurt
You or I will do

My teeth tremble
They let me in sometimes
Blood all around me

Fix me
I'll slink back into the dark
A convict

I'll forget you
Oh horror, oh terror
It aches inside

La Petite Morte

Beneath the swampy stars
Bewinged tuxedo ruffles,
Slinky black dress pulses fretfully.
Dewdrops for eyes
Pearly cheeks studded with husky kisses
Nails like barbed wire digging my back
God how I love you,
So pretty in your terror
The Red Planet radios me for genocide tonight
But I swear I won't hurt you

So many beautiful stars…
You can have them, every one of them,
Just close your eyes…
Your face, ghastly pale
Is rapturous in the moons giddy light,
Sweet lips pursed, dreading imminent kisses,
Sheaves of dark hair scattered around you,
Handful of roses creeping through the dark tresses
Your eyes, they seem so sad,
Like dispirited telescopes gazing into a blank sky.
Don't weep darling,
For you are the night.

Pumpkins frame the sore field,
Fearful of the carving knife.
Barren soil scratches beneath alluring elf-shoes
Nothing can console the mordant sky
I know God is dead as I smell your skin

Doll parts bend wearily
The stars in your eyes are all wrong
We could stay here together
Throwing knives like paper planes
Shriveled Dracula and little Mina,
Flesh dissolving to reveal slimy tendons and hollowed bones,
Skeleton lovers cuddling in a rotted pumpkin patch.

Your sordid smile stops my heart.
Flying saucers coast,
Seeking specimens.
Sawn-off, the shooter nuzzles my leg,
His bullets hungry for your cool flesh.
Please don't scream…

Compound eyes flex before the whip-crack of doting slaughter
Six hundred thousand years drift by on jerky puppet strings
In some tragic heaven, a bored God laughs
Spattered pumpkins guffaw in the fallow grass
Demons wail and hang from the rafters,
But they cease to matter in gun sights
Ah, the wind,
It whispers such horrendous nonsense…

My little one repose in my arms
Such a small world coming free
The stars, they are worthless without you…

Decimator

You lived
in a cherry red dollhouse,
dust bunnies and brown sugar mice;
that was the kingdom of sweetness
that bloomed in blissfulness,
ignorant of all that transpired
outside walls thin as gossamer.
You lived,
and were non the wiser.

You cried,
finding me drunk on darkness,
wings crumpled like fast food wrappers,
choking on dust with every pained breath.
You scrubbed my scales clean,
gave me a tree to sleep in
and fed me from a bowl.
You cried,
boundless affection sparkling in your eyes.

It stewed,
a Miltonic hellfire in my belly.
The pain was unbearable.
It bubbled and churned, bubbled and churned
until it blew out my sides,
and when you rubbed my back
I screamed like a cat.
It stewed,
and how could you know what lay in my scaly heart?

You crumbled
as my wings beat the dead air,
marshaling the aimless dust
into a desert wind, battering the hope and bliss
that defined that sweet kingdom.
I scattered the dust bunnies,
and banished the mice forever.
You crumbled
before the horror of my desolation song.

I scorched you
with the hellfire that had that had festered
in the scarred hollows of my heart
and could never be extinguished.
I laughed in a voice like static,
for you had found a sad, dying creature,
but never wondered why he was like that.
I scorched you,
laughing as a forgotten kerosene heater exploded.

I looked down at you
begging me to stop and let you soothe my agony
even as I sucked in your tiny sun,
crunched the hot glass
and swallowed the shards whole,
drool dripping from my mandibles,
and then that was the end of it all.
I looked down at you,
and I sneered.

I laughed
even as my own lungs burned,
and I spiraled down into the melting palace,

your sobs numbing me like alcohol
as I became one with the flames,
the liquefying plastic,
and the pall of your suffering.
I laughed,
and knew no more division as the darkness returned.

Danielle

Nothing kills her.
The psy-ops stole into her mind, and beheld the terror of her focus:
a kaleidoscopic storm of hunger, blood lust, rage, and at the heart of it all,
a pit of loneliness, all fused into a singularity of nuclear hatred for us,
cowering behind our missile launchers and machines of war.
The fire burns our city,
it scorches and destroys everything, and we can no longer tell
where her breath kindled
or where our firepower fell short of rupturing her hide.

I remember a September long ago, years before
we dug in the planet and awoke its mistress,
I used to write beautifully morbid poems like I was
some deviant freak. I liked the winter,
when the falling snow would make
anything worth objectifying for a few lines of verse.
There was a trapdoor in my heart,
and the air left my soul.
I filled it with black mold and the debauchery
that lurked in the writings of my heroes,
forgetting that Lovecraft, Poe, Baudelaire, and the rest,
preferred to stay indoors and let the terrors fester outside.

She shrieks to a sky that cannot hear her,
displays her ferocity to a city
that has fallen before her brutality.
Will we sorry few who may yet live
ever get her dreadful majesty out of our heads?
How can we simply forget the terrible wobble of her legs

as she waddled through buildings
already crumbling and melting from the heat of her wrathful heart?

I think fleetingly of God,
too tired to shed tears for the rest of the doomed wretches,
Atlantis, Pompeii, Dresden, Hiroshima, New York, Aleppo, etc,
and figure we've always willfully misunderstood our relationship with
existence.
I'm dying alone, and my destructor isn't even aware of me,
and if she were, my last piteous scream wouldn't even register.
Before the endless depths of her despair,
in the shadow of her agony,
the air crackles, the ground shakes, tension wires snap, asphalt melts,
tunnels collapse, libraries burn, cemeteries rupture, clouds burst and
bleed like pustules, and the earth is scorched bare.

Shame

I am he, the scaly one, venomous
wyrm who clutches the whole world in his coils.
My muscles are unforgiving, like thus:
caged tiger, millionaire, swollen boils.
We monsters, wolves, snakes, trolls, this is our place,
we strike dire terror in god and man alike,
rattling and spitting in their holy faces!
Eternal we dwell, songs written about our spikes.
And yet here am I, trapped beneath the waves,
waiting for a showdown long prophesied;
I live only to see the hero cave,
and my red eyes burn with malice unfreed.
Hunters, we are hunted, our lives a game,
and beaten, we swallow our tails in shame.

Surrender

Warm memories have I of the sunlight;
constant spring, joyous walks through lush gardens,
true friends, keen to sate my wolf's appetite,
and betrayal, a dismembering bite.
Honor my friends lacked not, and much of might;
how we battled in the snowlands, father
was always proud to see me, his shaggy son, fight.
His sly face, in love I smeared with slobber,
howling with rage when they called him "robber".
I grew, and the sky-world lost its splendor;
former friends leashed me, stabbed a sword in me,
and before their cruelty, I could only surrender.
I trot ahead of an army of dust,
and eat their sun; now, only night is just.

Drinking With Thor

"Raise your horns for brave fallen friends
We will drink tonight"
-Amon Amarth, "Raise Your Horns"

The storm clouds clash and destroy everything outside,
shielding giants and all manner of atrocities,
and who fucking cares?
I'm so drunk I don't even know
if Thor hears me yell
"Fuck it, there's no god anyway,
none of this matters!"
The tremor of his father hollering down from Heaven or Asgard or
whatever
barely fazes us as we down our glasses and slam them back on the bar
like John Henry hustling to beat his irrelevance back with two puny
hammers.
How fast can we drink ourselves into the lowest possible level of
consciousness?
How hard do we need to go before
we can escape the never-ending drudgery of daily life?
The thunder god tells me that
"Every day flows into the next without mercy,
I've lost so much
time
fighting everyone's wars,
accomplishing nothing,
years of my life poured away like oceans
spilling into nothingness,"
and I just laugh and order us another round,

gunfires, Jagerbombs, shots of tequila,
all the drinks I can slur before the bartender rolls her eyes
and grabs us two boilermakers, which we sad bastards seize,
breaking into a pathetic, degenerate duo of "Raise Your Horns"
as the night goes to hell and back
and my ignored phone buzzes and buzzes until it finally dies.
Drinking, I think of my biological father,
I only really know two things about him:
he drove a Harley Davidson like he was Easy Rider,
and whenever he realized what a meaningless void his life was
he'd mutter one word, like an incantation:
"Whatever".
Thor knows where my head is, and tells me
that we all become our fathers in the end,
grouchy and tired as winter,
seated on a throne you don't even want,
and there's no regret, just emptiness,
and you don't cry, because no one around you
can hear you,
you're meaningless, left behind,
throbbing with pain until you finally die.

Goetia

Bodily Contortions

I kneel on a yoga mat striped like a dragon,
struggling to keep my eyes off her
as she contorts like a demo
of all the things we do when we're together,
the cow pose,
reverse tabletop,
downward facing dog;
I keep my head twisted away from her,
as the pose demands.

A chill wind assaults us,
we young millennial, secular people
twisting our bodies into the shapes of Hindu gods,
our mats littering the warehouse like some damn commune.
We're like hermit crabs,
the shells of our parents withered traditions
slipping off our backs,
making way for us to slide into new ideas.
Pulling my hands to my heart's center,
I briefly wonder if we ever get free, and then
I catch her hungry glance.

The wind blows through the warehouse again, and
I sigh, because it's old Ymir,
the Ice-Man whose broken body
was crumbled up into a ball
and thrown into the rippling void
to become the world that we fester upon.
His broken bones are the mountains,

his hair forests, blood the oceans, and his cracked skull
the sky.
We are all just lice
in Ymir's hair.

We shiver and screw our bodies
into impossible shapes
and I ignore the passage of time,
waiting for the ordeal to end.
The pain is cathartic, as Vishnu or Shiva or Kali
or whoever intended,
but at this point,
I just want to pull my arm out from under my leg
and put it gently around my girl's neck;
I doubt those double jointed,
six-armed Hindu deities would appreciate it,
but old Ymir,
scrunched up in a ball,
missing the finer things in life,
I'm sure would concur.

Stitches

I am alone in the dark as the Ragdoll leaves my side
Worms squirm through me as she turns
A tentative goodbye swimming in her button eyes;
The door closes as she stands in her high-heels
Gazing at me as I stand in that ungodly hour
Fevered and uncertain over the tumultuous night.

Great moths overtake the moon as the colors fade
The sun is dead to me,
And the world seems a silent, black and white movie.
Clouds hang like blots of milk
Turning slowly within a darkened crystal ball;
Sweet rain pounds upon the dead corn,
Forlorn drops seeping through the thick stalks in vain,
Falling to their tiny deaths in the fallow dust.

Epitaph Street has never seemed so lifeless in the expressionist light;
I can taste coffin dust in the air,
And in a bar nearby, there's a banshee singing my name.
Doppelganger voices argue and cajole as I order a drink
Speaking of Ragdoll smiles and kisses that promised salvation.
Foaming at the mouth, dreaming of redemption,
I ignore the bitter reality broadcasted,
Still seeing the gritty opera through the delirious lenses
Only a poet or a madman would be able to make sense from.

Murmurs of deicide form in these frayed hours,
As smoke sifts from the last candle, drowning in its own wax,
The eternity where clocks stuck on midnight struggle to turn,

And asylums thrum with bad dreams as the medicine weakens.
My little lily is lost to me, still chaste, the petals sealed.
I lie on the roof, watching the crows as they circle for the carrion on
my bones.
Staring at the stars,
The twinkling fragments of a crystal rose, the boutonnière of some
dead god.
As the Sandman makes his stealthy approach,
I see the pattern for a moment,
The Ragdoll's smile stitched across the skyline,
And crawl back through my window
Awaiting the hiss of sleepy-sand to take me to the dank alleys
Where devils in pajamas wait behind trash can shadows
Eager to tear out my heart and twist it into a Ministry of Love
Where no benevolent darkness in which to snuggle can exist.

The Angel with the Hook in Her Lip

"Hold my hand, spin around,
hold my hand, spin around,
hold my hand, spin around
this is heaven upside down"
-Marilyn Manson, "Heaven Upside Down

I reek of coffee, and
I struggle from the rubble
of my apartment
only to be suffocated by
daylight.
It smothers my eyes,
clogs my throat,
and I feel
lucky to be driving away
to a job;

My phone buzzes,
and there's a text from
my boyfriend
that reads:
I long to smell your skin again, baby,
lets reboot heaven 2night

He's a vicious lover,
leaves grisly bruises
all across my breasts like
craters on the fickle face of the moon,
stretches me, cruciform

against the bed,
and smiles a crooked smile
as he goes inside,
and lifts me above all the nations of the earth
and whispers—

I cloister my phone
deep in my purse,
quarantined like a wayward daughter.
The uniformed vampires that
patrol my street with their swirly eyes
and hateful badges
pause as I dodge them
and cower in my room.

The world turns without
the sacrifice of my personal space.
Now I'm alone,
I'll meditate to flute music,
I'll muse over all my mistakes
I'll wait until my fickle moon
blooms to completion.

I tick nonstop,
a clock whose batteries never dry out.
My phone buzzes,
and I quiet its bees with a swipe.
The poison is slick
on the floor.
Cat vomit elucidates the squalid glory
of my home.
The jeans are too tight,
so I squeeze into them and

bite my lips.
There's only one thing
that can make my ticking stop.

I invite him in, and he
sinks his fangs into my neck.
I look into his eyes and gasp
"I love you,"
and he anoints me with a crown of horns
and rasps like a junkie scoring his smack
"I missed you, darling,"
as he slaps his onyx bracelets on me
and throws me on the floor.

"Let's reboot heaven," I say as
he falls on me like a mushroom cloud;
my clothes don't last a minute.
"We'll give it more moxie, spunk,
and less exposition," he replies, and then
he pushes the grotesque length of his manhood
down my throat
and fishes out my helpless soul
and nails it to the wall
so it doesn't blow away.

He peels back the skin
that isn't me,
and disassembles the skeleton
that isn't me,
and knolls the bones
that aren't me
like they're Legos,
and then puts it all back together.

He tears me out of the wall and inhales me,
devouring me into his infernal body,
I'm his sickness now, he quivers and sweats with my fever,
and when he kisses my hollow body,
I'm back on the floor, and he's spreading his wings.

"Not tonight,
my darkling one,"
I murmur, pulling him close,
dousing the spiraling flames in his eyes,
and curling up the sneer on his demon lips.
The claws are sharp, and the kiss is merciless,
and then he's gone
until the next time.

The Carfax Valentine

"If that were all, I would stop here where we are now, and let her
fade away into peace..."
- Bram Stoker, Chapter 12, *Dracula*.

The beeping machines taunted me,
("Immortality will always evade you,
for all mortal clay is damned.")
Trapped in the deadpan cell,
your charms withered in silent sorrow,
fading as the drugs and fear overwhelmed you.
The doctors in their white coats, they said I was sick,
but I would not let them take your agony from me.

I rescued you from their scalpels and syringes;
even in death you were so lovely,
mercy was the only thing I ever denied you.
Despite the pain, you refused to cry,
always so damned proud, my Allyson.

There was poetry in your suffering,
Rheumy irises glinting like black ice melting down,
the cadence of your spine as you squirmed,
pale lips grinding morosely in quiet torment.
You were so lonely in that terminal hour,
for I had gone away from you.
Watching you fail in my arms,
my devotion to you corroded to a gruesome lust.

Moonstruck, I lost my self
To my horror, I became
a smiling dog eager to consume your flesh,
to feel your bones snap like twigs in my hands,
to extinguish the morose specks in your eyes.
I would lose your love,
but only to seize the moon,
never to let it shrivel away,
our dystopia would be mine forever.

You sighed as I licked your cheek,
Never dreaming that my tenderness could be usurped.
The horror on your weak face drove me mad with desire

I was so hungry/never wanted to hurt you/could never give you up/
never lose you/warm Blood dripping from my beard/smooth skin
breaking under my teeth/half your face gone With a bite/grasping
your soft sweet guts through the hole in you/tail wagging/blood blood
Blood so much god damned blood/i reached inside and broke it/broke
you/my paws Raking your back as you screamed/and sobbed/and
fought/and hugged me for comfort…

I dug you a hole in the yard,
that you might lie at peace in the wet soil,
Beneath spotted mushrooms and sickly skies.
I now scrawl your eulogy on the walls,
frantically scribbling with shrinking crayons
of walks under silhouette trees and baleful stars,
standing atop sewer grates for warmth,
of raw kisses and lunar flesh,
uncensored affection given freely,
of ruined symmetry and discarded humanity,
chthonic hunger appeased without a thought.

Frost descends through the years,
scarring me with endless regret.
Nothing claws at my door,
no vengeful ghost rises to suck my blood;
swathed in perdition,
I paw through the snow and dirt,
a dog after his hidden bone.
I hug your tiny skull against my chest,
howling at the naked moon in sorrow.

Valkyrie Sunset

At the end I did for her as she did for me,
I stayed by her side,
singing to her softly as the shutters banged hollowly.
Her dreams were always the same,
horrific, splintered memories of a vast swamp wreathed in mist,
of blind spirits mumbling as they sank into the murk
a black avatar of despair fluttering,
calling her name in her father's voice.

I crushed her pills with a spoon, and later
we shared a milkshake as she cried
and I drank deeply of the cup,
tasting her fallen tears in the ice-cream and cold milk.
Starved wolves raised their voices that day,
and I felt sick to my heart as I messed her hair,
my watch was ticking beneath a mound of clothes.

Beneath me, she paused, mid-breath,
to rattle,
then she was no more.
I wrapped her in the sheet,
and kissing her pale cheek,
left her to lie between the mildewed walls.

I watched the sun set from the roof,
remembering last summer,
holding her hands as we spun in the daisies, a golden age lost forever.
Black birds swarmed through the open window,
and I thought of her as she was then,

laid out for those fat crows,
her arm hanging limply off the side of the bed,
black bands under her eyes,
naked toes sticking out of the white sheet,
bones buried beneath a shallow layer of skin.

Fading light, falling sun, withering day,
(Petite skeleton picked clean)
Warmth was giving way to emaciated moonlight
(She's all around now)
I strode through thin trees
(Exodus of crows cawing at me)
Calling to the wolves to claim me,
(Their engorged bellies hurt hurt hurt)
But they had turned on each other,
(HURT)
And they were all dead,
(HURT UNTO DEATH)
Dead like the daylight,
(Can't be, can't be, can't be, not that same fate)
Like my Madonna
(Our flesh fermenting in the same bile)
Dead, dead, dead,
(No respite from the pain, no escape from her passing)
Gone from me forever.
(Not even in the promise of dying.)

Catharsis

"And if your head explodes with dark forebodings too
I'll see you on the dark side of the moon"
-Pink Floyd, "Brain Damage"

"Father, I have sinned."
My brethren hide in their pews-
"Please, I seek forgiveness for my sins."
Clean-shaven, love-lorn, moon-sick, flesh-crazed-
"I consorted with sinners, for I am a sinner also."
Cannibals, they want nothing of the desiccated skin of a dead lord,
only-
"I want the glory of God in my life;"
To sing the praises of the moon, of the night, of the stars, of the cold
and the hunt, to-
"My soul is ruined,"
Howl and fight over road kill, to pray for snow and war, the end of all
things;
"And I want only to be whole and pure once more,"
Augmented reality to stunt the cycle, burning wheels fill our hidden
souls,
"Complete and beautiful in the grace of God once more."
May Fenrir have mercy on you all.

The mimes motion from their sewer-grates
powerless to escape;
the sky, Batman-blue,
is soulless and moony,
perfect catalyst for mass hysteria.
Priests skulk in the shadows like thin black bats,
chewing crackers as they sanctify their murdered god.

The city, this drab city of crosses, huddles beneath the august cloak
of a horror it can no longer remember.

I watch my love in our bed,
content on this night, this forgotten holiday,
her attention glued not to hammering boards over windows,
but to the worthless television,
curled up in bed in a t-shirt and panties,
her hair strewn down her face like black auroras;
how I long to end this winter of suppression,
cast their saints from their pedestals and retake the night,
but for her, I do nothing, for her love sustains me,
and I would not lose her trust,
even at the price of my own salvation.

You know my love like no one else ever will,
so look into my eyes like you love to,
and hear my heart crying from an alleyway tonight.
Touch me, hug me, kiss me,
hear the stars screaming deafeningly,
bone spurs ripping through my tissues;
So hard to look in your pure face sometimes,
not worthy of your love,
but I'll take it all the same.

Titans' roar through the tearing of your clothes
I'll anoint them in cricket dust when they come for me.
Swan-colored, the moon yawns outside our window,
a monstrous, silver bimbo flaunting her body before our doorstop,
she wants me, hungers for the adoration I give you,
but she is trapped in the obsidian sky,
and you are clasped in my arms,
soft, lovely, pale, mine.

Stained glass depicts
Dark mythologies
But the glass is thin
When it breaks
My brethren will crawl
Through the shards
Free the sky
Unleash their feral spirits
And I will watch the venerated sky
And sob for the comfort
Your freckles gave me in the dark
But for a while longer
Our skin remains smooth

Awakening the next morning,
daylight smites my betrayer's eyes feebly,
pink clouds throb like arteries in the sky,
and the wind speaks in labored breaths,
hissing fallow threats and beseeching me to return.
I swear I can hear the mimes chanting.
They try to warn those above in hopes of clemency,
but their words are gibberish to the daywalkers.
I long for a silver bullet to end this paralyzing fear,
catch me sweetie,
I'm always falling in my dreams.

Cheering as they burn the heathens,
mumbling beneath the great crucifix,
throwing my holy books into their furnace,
perhaps this is the end of things,
the wolf-age, the axe-age,
and you, you are my tragic Ligeia,
destined to depart this world as the catharsis breaks at last,
the fireflies whirling around you in a skull-marked chora
impending death written in the stars above you.

Dirt

I smelled the falling rain through the soaked dirt
The trees drank greedily
So happy to be alive
Shedding their bark
Their throbbing roots growing through my stolid body
White and naked
Hiding from shifting realities
Unable to understand the agonies of my comprehension
In my hatred for boxes
I buried myself in the dirt
No one would remove my memories through the brain surgery I
wanted
("Listen buddy,
Just take this bone saw
And cut along the dotted line!")
I knew it wasn't a real place,
That golden city with the rainbow bridge,
Those fucking Viking lords with their goddamn giant axes
Damn it all.

Ex Nihilo.
It's funny how a period adds gravity to a sentence, like it's an anchor,
Tying a colossal idea to a fixed point,
Or giving a definite end to an eternal concept,
Right?
I used to pretend fictional worlds didn't exist
But now I know better.

Hunting Moortails at night,
I felt the first pangs of futility

Seeing all of the dead things I used to mark the road
I understood much of the dark and of myself
I was the dark
I was the void
I was the destroyer
I was the hater
I was the jerk
I was the devil
I needed-

-you-

Understanding fully of course,
That redemption could be bought with a twitch of the wheel
And I would join the glassy-eyed things on the road.

Darling, do you remember
The first thing I said to you?
You never knew of the tears I threatened to shed that day,
Crushed in the dirt for so long,
Escaping my pain,
You saved me from my mouthful of beetles and dirt,
The loneliness of my grave (and also my life),
And showed me that the sunlight would not destroy me;
Now all the world is white noise to me,
For in your arms the struggling dimensions all come together,
and normalcy seems possible.

Smiling Through the Pain

"And in your garments that exhale your perfume
I would bury my aching head,
And breathe, like a withered flower,
The sweet, stale reek of my love that is dead."
-Charles Baudelaire, "Lethe."

The sun was lost in the tie-dye sky that day
when she was crying over the last glass of milk;
trading saliva for what was left of the spoiled sugar in my heart,
wipe it up with that white sheet you ripped out of me,
It's just my soul.
Don't look too deeply into it now
Not without your domino mask…

I killed the singing birds when they lamented the overdosed sky
from under her as she trapped me with her spider legs;
she asked me when it was ok for her to scream,
and every day when her dark-seeded skin left me,
I died with a smile,
never wanting to live in a reality
where I was forced to go without her heroin in my life…

The colors were washed out when the insipid sunlight found its way
home and you jumped for joy at the return of the normal light;
our dance partners changed too fast for us to think,
spinning too fast to ever fall in love again.
I saw you and you said goodbye with a smile
even though you still came home every night
and gleefully tore me from my pitiful costume…

The colors were all gone the next day when you
called me a beast for stealing your purity;
twisted your innocence and made you like me,
only to run when I asked you to become the monster's bride.
Tasting grounds in my coffee,
I knew how your face would
look when you told me I was too sad…

The majesty was gone when those feminine aliens fixed the sky,
breaking my heart as butterflies came into focus,
no longer biomorphic shapes;
and I faced you for the last time perhaps,
drenched in pale lamplight.
There was no real conclusion
just a hasty explanation excusing everything.

Hurling myself at the walls that I might wear myself down and
escape the daylight,
I missed the carnival colored days when we were all so happy and
life was simple,
Before those things broke it all,
The haggard witches and their mindless war;
I long to be safe under cover of night beside my Juliet calling out
"Chastity, chastity, wherefore art thou?"

Kill For Her

My dark goddess,
she wore the moon on her forehead,
and plucked her harvest
from the men we brought her
drinking in the menarche of the night.
None could resist her,
but who in our freezing land would?

She was our true Queen,
driven out by the whispering stone priests,
and hunted like a mad saber-cat.
Her dread hunger we rued,
but her red smile,
wide in mesmeric moonlight
we longed for,
pining like little children.

Her den we found,
guarded by rude pikes
and yellow-eyed fiends,
who devoured my fur-clad friends.

"What right hast thou?"
the millennial seraphs cried out
as I drove them before me,
howling in terror of the flames I wielded.

For this, the Queen emerged
from her black hole in the rock

and bit her lip.
I marveled at the red foam
that so beautifully hung there,
like a dream, and then she
plucked me from the earth—

Now I hunch in the dark
and gnaw my dry bones,
silent as a crab,
only the coarseness
of my claws scraping against the cave wall
wounding the solitude of my exile.
I paint her slowly, adding pigment from
flowers, sediment, and blood
collected in crude stone bowls.

Her hair I trace from obsidian powder,
tracing her smoky black tresses
until they form a cloud of soot,
swathing her face.
Her body I compose from bone dust,
smearing the stuff with my hands,
lovingly stroking the wall
the way I long to stroke the very hips
and arms I create.
The mouth is a gash of blood,
dabbed across her heart-shaped face,
and her eyes
peer from her lustrous, dragon-blackened hair
with a greenness spilled from plant stems,
broken in their prime.

I admire my work by the withering firelight,
but I find it lacking.
There is no breath to make her heavenly breasts rise
and fall,
and her eyes, for all their sparkling sea glass,
lack the verdant glory that ripples there.
When I close my eyes, I see the true roundness of her hips,
a perfect geometry that my pathetic art
could never hope to replicate.

The twilight majesty of death's late kingdom
is mine to wander now,
following in the wake of my laughing Queen,
treading the hot trails she leaves in the snow.
I kill for her,
and from high up in the mountains
I howl with the shaggy beasts
so that all can hear, and
this world of dull men
and blunt priests
will remember our Queen's promise
that when her phantom is slain and forgot
the ice will melt
and the mammoths will all perish.

Devilgotchi

The Summoning

Magic, it feels so dumb,
light the candles, draw the circle,
(drawn with white chalk, found in the local Dollar Tree)
place the black scrying mirror
(inexpensive, purchased on Etsy from a nice lady with a witchy
username)
on the wall I'll be facing,
pour the incense and pick the sigil
(burned into a wooden disk by yours truly, Sorcerer Supreme)
flick off the lights, and then, well,
sit down in the circle,
(simple and white, no pentagram, we aren't looking to trap any
spirits)
lotus position like the Bodhisattvas of yore,
and meditate, muttering low
Tasa Alora Foren Astaroth.
I said magic felt so dumb,
but I don't mean stupid,
I mean dumb, mute, nearly meaningless,
as I sit in the dark, smelling the pretty incense,
mumbling nonsense words,
thinking about how
Joe Kelly and John Dee
scammed the Queen of England with a crystal ball
and some chicken scrawl;
"Enochian letters, the alphabet of the angels," they called them,
and the rest is history. Just ask anyone interested in this stuff
instead of their local church or mosque.

Tasa Alora Foren Astaroth
these Enns are probably the same thing,
nonsense words scribbled by a medieval con-artist
looking to get laid and paid like ol' Mister Crowley.
I open one eye to peek at the scrying mirror,
its glossy black face reflecting back the candlelight
the way a magic mirror should,
but no malign face peers back.
The candles burn without incident, untroubled by
any ethereal presence.
The incense is unappreciated by anyone not *moi*,
and I feel pretty fucking ridiculous.
All this money and effort, and not even a cracked mirror.
No Lovecraftian whispers in alien tongues,
Poe-esque visions to drive me mad,
heck, not even a Stephen King-like tightening of my balls,
just an idiot sitting alone in a circle,
performing a ritual like a Christian.

Tasa Alora Foren Astaroth.
I mutter it a few more times, but my concentration is lost.
My eyes snap open, and my meditation is at an end.
I hunger for a late night snack,
something prosaic, basic, normal,
I've got cold chicken, coffee cake, even
cereal and almond milk. Hey, some Earl Grey might even suffice,
bitter tea to wipe away the disappointment
of being stood up by the Archduke of Hell.
The kitchen light is on, and to my shock,
a little man with scaly skin
and red Crocs on his chicken feet
(and are those my fucking boxers?)
is standing by the fridge, drinking my milk
right out of the goddamn carton.

Disappointment on Riot's Eve

The world seemed to be on fire.

David Bowie, Chester Bennington, Prince, Chris Cornell, and Prin-
cess fucking Leia all died.
A horrible, narcissistic goblin sat in the White House for almost four years,
bringing with it all the nastiness that putting a monster on a throne entails.
Treaties disrupted, economies crashed, minorities targeted, wars
threatened;
A new and improved corona virus surfaced like a vengeful curse,
causing every governor and Jewish mother
to impose quarantine lest we all get sick with a super flu and die
(the goblin president didn't believe the virus was all that big a deal,
couple o' thousands o' dead folks, eh, whateva);
A black man was killed by a police officer who kneeled on his neck
for nine minutes,
heedless
to the man's pleas of
"I can't breathe"
and the entreaties of countless onlookers
who watched him die.
Protests began around the country,
despite of the deadly corona virus.
I suppose people were sick of being locked indoors,
stewing in their post-job-layoff afterglow,
without even a decent bar to go blow their stimulus on,
and then,
probably worst of all
I tried to make things better by summoning a demon,
and instead of some terrifying lord of Hell with hordes of bloodthirsty

monsters at his beck and call
and the sanction of the Great Satan to grant all my seething wishes,
I got you, some petulant imp
with no agenda beyond
blackmailing me and stealing my internet like a
filthy teenager.
This whole shit-show really upends my dreams
of turning into a Luciferian weirdo at thirty;
I should have stuck with chaos magic and the Tarot like Alan Moore.
At least then I wouldn't need a middleman
to bring down my mania
so I could finally feel as low and hurt

as all that burning world out there does.

The Storm

On the fifth day of the riots in Philadelphia,
the storm arrived. It smote police officers standing beside
idle armored vehicles blocking exists and cross-streets,
and pelted choppers hovering like malevolent dragonflies,
staring down at congregations of protesters
and mobs of looters alike; the broken glass
of a small bookstore called Shakespeare and Co. shone like diamonds
as the winds twisted and tore like the claws of ravenous ghosts,
unchained to avenge themselves finally.
My phone buzzed savagely, a TORNADO WARNING
urged me to click it as rain pellets banged against my window like the
William Tell Overture.
I hear massive booming sounds outside,
and on the internet
people whisper rumors about escaped tigers and
cop cars with sonic guns mounted on them
to dissuade people from joining
the human storm
once the tornado warning is past.

Seventy-Five Year Old Man

They threw a seventy-five year old man to the ground and
kept moving, maintaining the integrity of their line
of black-clad, baton-clutching, armored riot-cops,
marching like a legion of armored knights
securing spoils of war after a victorious sweep.
The seventy-five year old man's head struck the pavement
where he lay as if he were dead,
a pool of dark blood forming below his brow
like a long, gentle sigh.
Two riot-cops were suspended from the force,
one for shoving the seventy-five year old man,
the second for making the first
keep moving when he considered
stopping to help him,
bleeding his consciousness out on the pavement.
Fifty-seven other riot-cops on that force
resigned in protest;
the two riot-cops were just following orders,
maintaining the line they insisted,
protecting the city,
never clarifying on just who exactly
they were protecting it from.

The Hypocrite's Wish

There are so many morons on the internet who think summoning
demons
is like calling a new best friend out of an imaginary
(totally not hell)
abyss
to just like, hang tight and agree with all their tepid beliefs before
asking for a simple favor, assuming that it doesn't cost them anything simple
like their immortal soul,
but then again,
who isn't in debt for the rest of their lives at this point?
Revolutions are the same way.

It seems romantic, incredible,
change your standing in society and countless lives
with just a simple gesture.
With enough moxie and hope,
any man could be Robespierre.

I feel like those scrubs on Reddit, all
styling themselves as some new breed of limp-wristed
Aleister Crowley clone, as
half-baked as their sad, post-modern, "New Age" nonsense:

"Is Leviathan my patron?
in the last couple of days, I think of nothing but Leviathan,
whilst practicing meditation and reciting His Enn
my heart pounds in my chest, I feel jittery.
He came to me in dreams, at least I think so,
I knew it was him because

of the strong and overwhelming feeling that enveloped my entire body.
Perhaps I am thinking too much into it,"
says one poster,
sounding like a Catholic describing an encounter with the Holy Spirit.

The comments are no better:
"Maybe try to invoke and ask him?
Like people, you'll probably want to date (interact with) a few demons
before settling down with one for the rest of your life."

"Hail Prince Seere!" exclaims another post,
reading like a goddamned Glassdoor review.
"I would like to take this opportunity to thank Prince Seere for
helping me get the job I wanted.
The interview went well
and they ended up calling me only a few hours after!
Prince Seere worked very fast and provided good results."
Like, did these people give up on traditional religion simply because they felt
Yahweh was really unconcerned with their petty issues?

The demon loafing on my couch is unmoved by my pettiness.
"They're happy, aren't they?
Their play-acting gives them a bigger dopamine rush
than all those beers you wasted, pouring them out
while chatting with a non-existent Odin
like you could lure him down from his celestial mountain.
And hey man, that one kid even got a job out of it!"

You don't see an issue with this?
All their holy books are self-published, made up drivel,
and if those morons actually summoned something like you,
you'd ruin any hopes they might have with the supernatural.
It's one thing if Satan never taps you on the shoulder

while you're meditating;
you'd be surprised what people hallucinate
when they're all alone
and their minds are singularly focused,
fixated day and night on manifesting their reality
through intoxication, meditation, or good old isolation,
until one night the obsession and mental [devastation] training
tunes them to the right mental station and
Behold! The bane of Gilgamesh, foe of Yahweh
and the one true Lord of This World,
the Bull of Heaven stands before you,
bidding you go forth and
tell that cute brunette you think she's kind of neat.

Thus is summoning nothing justified.
But what if one of these foolish Redditors summons you?
Here I sit, conversing with a representative of
the Demonic Divine on my couch,
and I'm dismayed to see that he's nothing special.
I might as well actually just see a psychiatrist
or play the fucking lotto than fiddle with this magic shit.
What good are you?

The demon grins, my last seltzer can in his hand
as he transforms,
taking on an aspect of terrifying grandeur.
"You've given me my due,
entertaining me with your spastic hypocrisy,
and not bothering to try to banish me back
to my regal subterranean tower
as I indulged in your pathetic human pleasures
and challenged your feeble atheism
as you teeter on the edge of madness,

puzzling over my existence and what it portends,
I, the foul angel Asteroth, Duke-Worm of the Infernal Sphere,
offer you one wish, one favor before I depart."

Something, Anything

Duke Astaroth waits patiently.
I didn't think making a wish would be this abrupt,
or that I would have an infernal genie with an already
low opinion of me
judging me with deep-set, coal-red eyes.

I think of the chaos raging outside, the pain and the hurt
and the fear of the brave protesters,
whom I've done nothing to aid, for all my
post-Asatru, anti-New Age, Nietzsche-quoting, Thorite blustering,
and I kneel, uttering the words:

"Great Astaroth, rid this city of cops.
Make it so that no unarmed person
dies while the protesters demonstrate,
and the tear gas and rubber bullets
are as ineffective as
flowers placed in gun barrels."

Seated atop his stinking dragon,
the demonic prince flew through the rain-drenched summer air,
smiting every police vehicle blocking exits, and
blowing those anxious officers awaiting the breaking of tension
out of the city with a caustic, eastern wind
cast from his left hand.
Batons and riot shields swirled in the maelstrom,
torn from the hands of armored goons
and left at the feet of those wielding nothing more harmful
than hand drawn signs begging for justice

and exhausted cellphone batteries, giving brief life
to windows for the world to witness
their defiantly non-violent resistance to the modern age.

And so it began, average people policing their own neighborhoods.
They met in Malcolm X Park and discussed methods of de-escalation,
established free food co-ops and education circles,
creating an aura of a socialist utopia,
until a well-meaning lady mentioned reparations,
and someone else lost their life
attempting to blow up an ATM machine with a stick of dynamite.

And true to his word, Astaroth kept the police out of the city
as armed men in masks (there was still a pandemic, after all)
began to charge businesses a fee for their protection,
and then
the first dissident to the new order was shot by a concened citizen
doing his duty.

Devilgotchi

"Why don't you ask the kids at Tienanmen Square?
Was fashion the reason why they were there?"
-System of a Down, "Hypnotize"

My wish led to an anarchist pipe dream;
I didn't think banishing all police through,
now we've got
trucks filled with white-supremacist psychos coming,
driving to immanetize the eschaton of their civil culture war.
What a year ago was fought over the politics of Star Wars and
superhero junk
over internet forums
will now be argued with bullets and cracked skulls.

I begged Astaroth to take the wish back, to
let the police restore order; I do not recognize
these black vehicles, or these socialist minutemen,
who eye me warily as I trace the pentagram and runic formulae
around the screen of a black Tamagotchi
under the light of the full moon.
Better the Devil you know
I reason,
but the demon has been freed to wreak his havoc
at my command.
I was as unqualified to summon a demon
as these angry activists who never won a single election
are to give us a better world.

I hold the Tamagotchi like a badge, pointing its
defaced shell at the demon as he looms between clouds,
maintaining the circle of protection around the city.
I speak the spell of banishment,
with a slight alteration.
Rather than being dispelled to his realm,
Astaroth finds himself encased in a tiny
digital, two-dimensional prison,
clutched in my hand, awaiting my justice
as his power vaccuum is dispelled.

Our dreams were bigger than our stomachs,
we must catch the devils we let out
and put them back in our pockets,
and roll up sleeves to confront the real problems.
Nothing can be fixed with wishful thinking,
the desperation to do anything.

The Whaler

The Whaler

Crucify me high,
dig the nails in
and turn my head
towards the sun.

The ocean is endless;
the restless souls of all men
can find respite, adventure,
and a dark grave here.

We are harpooneers,
we raise our voices and sing
for the wheeling sea birds,
the bloody foam on the waves.

The end of empire shadow
of my Father's kingdom
looms far, far from here;
imperial torments hold no sway.

There's no problem
a harpoon well-thrown won't solve
when all your problems are whales,
and I'm most adept at slaying beasts.

I'm free of it now,
my worst problem—
a chunk of metal that stormed in my hands,
and dripped with the blood of monsters,

I threw that heavy thing
into the cold abyss of the ocean,
and down it sank,
swallowed by whispering waves.

Listen for my voice,
ye anxious ones, on the dark horizon
I'll watch for a silver stream,
and ignore the dark face of the water.

Siderophobia

"Is it bright where you are?"
-Smashing Pumpkins

Shadow of starlight
kisses my heavy face
just like the galaxies of dust motes
swirling about the deck like
souls that have lost their homes.
What we do in the day and night
is permanent, irreversible,
leaves marks no witch can soothe away,
punctures the soul so it can float
no more. I sit alone on this deck,
harpoon-scarred and stained by old blood,
and gaze at the morning star,
shining brilliantly in a night sky that despises its luster.
The bold star dares its lessers
to snuff it out, and I long
for a touch of its defiant brilliance.
I dropped my heart in the ocean
like it was a penny,
payment for a quiet, lonely burial at sea;
but now I'm mortal and tired,
and long to fly through the stellar garden once more,
haunted no more by the sentient shimmer of whale eyes,
weighed down no more by a red anguish
that dulls my thunder, and drives me
to try and shun the razor-thin-crowned stars,

able only to observe them from a sullen distance,
while the world helplessly spins,
spellbound by stellar gravity.

Whale-Killer

The sunlit waters will soon be calm.
We kill the beast with pointy sticks,
keeping pace with the silver stream
of saliva seething into the turbulent waves
as the creature sobs in pain and terror.

It's a glorious day.
We go to our grim work,
our harpooneers' hands never twitching
as the sea birds wheel and raise their voices,
drowning out the funereal cries of the sea-bull.

The others on the ship raise the bloated thing
from the oceanic space its body was made for,
the hooks suspending it beside the ship,
a trophy as grisly as any I brought home,
a giant as powerful and beautiful as any I have slain.

They rob our kill of its meat and blubber,
but I care nothing for all that.
The glory is in
the sunlight bouncing off the harpoon's tip,
seasalt dripping from my wild-fire red beard,
the perfect throw, my only throw,
piercing the dying whale's heart.

Leviathan

I never choke on the detritus I swallow,
but now I feel a grim weight as I suck deep
the bounty of the black sea.

The weight of an ocean presses against my cyclopean muscles
as the stars in my tail tear blistering comets across the face of the deep.
My great belly scrapes against massive steel ships,
lost a century back and forgotten,
the unimaginable pressure flattening them like
the useless garbage they are.

There is another world
far, far above;
I streak for it, rising like a juggernaut
the dark rushing past,
the water breaking before the titanic bow of my snarling face.

I crash through the surface,
hurtling like a wrathful missile
thrown from the heart of the ocean's
freezing contempt,
to gulp the fresh, pure air,
gasping even as it burns
the red-laced billows of my lungs.

I fall,
peering once again into black vistas,
an endlessly silent, abyssal kingdom broken only by other shapes
as massive and indomitable as my own,

and secrets that no other creature,
be he fish, porpoise, or man,
shall ever be privy to,
for into my cthonic maw they are drawn,
the skeletons of giants,
the plunder of lost kingdoms,
and weapons cast aside by gods.

I am she who swims alone;
my ribs could cage the stars if ever they were pulled from my chest,
and my blood would drown the world in my seething fury.
The vault of my heart is a throbbing dungeon of monstrous echoes,
and the mallet I swallowed was too great a burden.
I upraise a tortured song that echoes through all the vastness of the
sea,
awakening the sleeping krakens and sea-gods of old from
beneath mounds of coral and broken ships
with the thunder and pain I extoll,
echoing like a sunken bell.

The Fighter

“Jove is my brother;
Mine eyes are the lightning;
The wheels of my chariot
Roll in the thunder,
The blows of my hammer
Ring in the earthquake!”
-Henry Wadsworth Longfellow, “The Challenge of Thor”

I tie the knots, roaring back as the squall
buffets me, wrestles me with its girth of water.
A foe mightier and more ancient I have never faced,
but I hold strong, for I am the storm incarnate.
Any man will I drink under the table,
any beast, no matter how gruesome,
will meet its end at the thunderous cracking of my knuckles,
and woe to any villain who betrays my trust.
I have crushed mountains beneath my warhammer,
and drank oceans to win drinking games against monsters.
Shall some earthly storm challenge the rival of Jove?
Verily, I say thee nay!

But see, my fellow sailors,
Ho!
Their world is ending,
look how they scramble
to battle the storm.
Girded in thick coats and hefty boots,
they lash the tiller and secure the sails,
howling against the bellowing wind

as they strive to ignore their friends
claimed by the heartless ocean.
Months of slaying whales
has brought this tension point
on which everything hangs in balance
against the savagery of the storm.
Should we fail to save the ship
or lose our barrels of oil
the ocean's greedy eddy will feast on our souls,
swallowing those cast overboard
or those drowning themselves in despair.

The waves are too great, the ship's timbers,
they strain as the ship is buffetted, and we are
engulfed in the salty wrath of the angry sea.
For all my boasting, I lose my footing,
and am saved only be the sacrifice of another man, who
gripping a rope, catches me, not stopping to consider what he is risking.

The waves fall away and the ship is tossed helplessly,
and as lightning arcs across the sky,
I see the arbiter of the storm.
A loathsome creature, she shrieks as she turns over and over,
driving the ocean mad with her convulsions,
her bright fins baiting the agitated wind as she crests and falls,
boring holes in the sea, battering our ship
with shock waves.

Old Stormalong

"Then they took Jonah and threw him overboard, and the raging sea
grew calm."
-Jonah 1:15

Pain in her eyes
in her voice
the lightning above
the seething waters below.
It is pain we experience,
the pain of a sunken goddess,
her jaw cracked by her own child,
and her gore painted across the firmament.
She was erased from the memory of the world,
and suffocated beneath the waters they poured
over her eviserated body.
The ocean was her tomb, her palace, and
though eons of ocean-gods and sea serpents and sunken islands
and submarines and lost ships and drowned sailors
fell to fossilize and join her in dreamless death,
she knew nothingness and no one sought for
the bones of her primordial grace.

"Until, fleeing from the gravity of my life and my responsibility,
I cast my mystical hammer,"
so heavy that only one as strong as myself could lift it,
into the sea, where I believed it would be forgotten forever.
Lightning scores the sky above, and now
I scream as I never screamed before,
a ship full of sailors behind me

as I fall into the black waters below

into the maw

of the goddess

and seize the powerhead

I carelessly threw down her throat

into her gentle heart

and pray to forces greater than I

that my sin can be forgiven.

9 789388 319218